TI WORTH-SHIP MANDATE

Perceiving The Ministry Of Worship

To Glenn x Jen:
Compliments of the
Season

B[illegible]
18.12.19.

THE WORTH-SHIP MANDATE

Perceiving The Ministry Of Worship

Rebecca Osei-Edwards

Foreword by Rev. Dickson Tuffour Sarpong

The Worth-Ship Mandate

Published by
Sophos Books
2 Woodberry Grove
London
N12 0DR
Sophos Books is a publishing imprint of Sophos Media Ltd.

Unless otherwise stated, all scripture quotations are taken from the King James Version of the Bible.
Verses marked NKJV are from the New King James Version
Verses marked NIV are from the New International Version
Verses marked NLV are from the New Living Version
Verses marked MSG are from The Message Bible

ISBN 978-1-905669-63-9

Cover design by *Icon Media*
Printed in the United Kingdom

CONTENTS

DEDICATION

These pages are inscribed with a special place
in my heart for My Father in heaven –
He found me worthy of His WORSHIP.

To Mom and Dad.
Neither of them wrote a book,
but they had loads embedded inside them!
A special one for Mother, now resting securely in
the arms of the Secret Keeper, for consistently
taking me to church. That's why I am here!

To my precious GIFTS:
Benedicta, Joseph and Princessa,
your love for God motivates me to do more.

To my husband, friend, shepherd,
big brother and counsellor: Isaac.
God has used you in many ways to shape my
calling.

ACKNOWLEDGEMENTS

Thank you, Rev. Martin Ossei, founder and senior Pastor of *Joyhouse London* and Apostle Jennifer Abigail Lawson-Wallace, founder and International President of *Women in Tune* and convenor of *Quiver Prayer Movement* respectively; for your proofreading and valuable advice on this project.

My pastors, Rev. Edwin and Beatrice Donkor; thank you for your endorsement. Rev Isaac Osei-Edwards, my co-labourer; my praise and worship friends, Pastors Isabella Ogo-Uzodike and Jojo Immanuel-Lawson; thank you immensely for reviewing aspects of the manuscript.

To Rev. Dickson Sarpong, *ICGC Jesus Temple ER* (Ghana), thanks for reading through the manuscript and offering to write a foreword. To Lady Lucy Sarpong, thanks for your nurturing in the Lord's vineyard. Shadowing you in my early years of ministry helped me to become a *'praiseful'* daughter of Zion.

Bishop Fred and Esther Apenteng, Rev. Dr. Kwasi Sampong, Rev. Kofi and Harriet Othere, Rev. Kate Ossei; thanks for your diverse support in my *'worshipful'* journey!

To my editorial consultant and publisher, Pastor Tokunbo Emmanuel, CEO of *Sophos Media Ltd.*, for pushing me to do my best! Your passion for excellence in the writing ministry is much appreciated. Congratulations for being the carriage that drove *The Worth-Ship Mandate!*

To my pastor friends: Rev. Moses and Nana Agyemang Asare, Rev. Samuel and Thess Asante Wiafe, Rev. Foster Ofori Temeng, Dr. William and Begay, Rev. Samuel and Ellen Akoto, Rev. Asante Dankyi and Priscilla, Rev. Dr. Bernard and Safoa Otopah Appiah, Dr. Eben and Sophia Adu, Rev. Ruth Tiso, Rev. Jennifer Prah, Rev. Mark Abban, Rev. Fred and Millie Ashong, Pastor Joe and Patience Anokye, Pastor Laud and Helena Fleisher, Pastor George and Vinnie Quaicoe, Pastor Felix and Christie

Tettey, Pastor Ebow and Martha Sagoe, Pastor Frank and Kukua Brobbey, Pastor Andy and Miriam Tawiah, Pastor Sam and Naana Mends Buer, Pastor Sam and Ann-Phylis Ofori, Pastor Yinka and Bibian Afuwape, Pastor Paapa and Mary Anderson, Apostle Williams and Antoinette Nana Agyei, Apostle Elijah-Ben and Coleen Agyapong, Pastor Jackie Magloire; my interactions with you at diverse times created various avenues for improving my knowledge in the SCHOOL OF WORSHIP. Thank you!

To my extended family: Siblings – Esther, Philip and Samuel; and in-laws, especially, my 'mother in love' and prayer partner, Mama (Deaconess) Mary Osei; you have been my life coach since I married your son!

Finally, to co-leaders: Deac. and Mrs Oblitey, Minister and Mrs Hagan, Minister and Mrs Addae and all members of *ICGC Potter's Temple*, South London, my local church; Your love for God, and belief in your pastor and I, gave me the peace of mind to complete this project.

Let praises rise!

ENDORSEMENT

Worship, as a concept, and its practice, remains an enigma to many well-meaning Christians. This is the result of ignorance and various misconceptions.

The fall of Adam, and the loss of God's glorified life in him, has led to humanity misinterpreting and perverting God's truth about many things, including true worship.

Lady Minister Becky's journey of faith in God and her passionate search for truth in worship, have culminated in this enlightened revelation of the righteous meaning and emphasis the Father accords true worship. God has a great and expectant desire for true worshippers, and the knowledge for excellent participation has been laid bare and made plain to every diligent enquirer and seeker, in this book.

The content of this book is revelation given by God to an author whose love, devotion, skill and experience before God's altar have produced this important spiritual resource for the Body of Christ.

Be blessed as you carefully read through the pages of this extraordinary book.

Rev. Edwin Donkor
Regional Overseer, ICGC Europe and North America
Senior Pastor, ICGC Kings' Temple London.

FOREWORD

Becky, as I affectionately call her, has been a music addict all her life! Growing up as a believer, she has always grabbed any opportunity given to her to minister a song or lead congregational worship. Truly, I can attest to the fact Lady Rebecca has a great call to the ministry of worship. This is an amazing woman with a mission, and I commend her for this excellent work done for the kingdom. The title of this book, *The Worth-Ship Mandate,* sends a myriad of signals about the depth of revelation to expect from reading it.

Some decades ago, practising as a worship pastor, I had come across this word 'worth-ship' which revolutionised my thinking about the concept. Yet, I had always hoped that someone would research biblical truths and explore the topic to benefit the wider body of Christ. Thankfully, Rebecca has now done that!

In this book, the author begins by setting the records straight on what worship is not. Wow! If worship is not the songs, instrumentation or the arts, then what is it? Contrary to the plethora of misconceptions people hold about the concept, Rebecca is emphatic about the relationship between the worshipper and the Creator, and considers this as the core of worship. The aspects of art and skill are only the means to worship.

This is indisputably true, because many people sing and never touch the heart of the Father at all. The art is mostly exalted above pure, intimate relationship with the Father. This is mainly due to how the art has been taught over and above the development of a personal love relationship with Jesus our Saviour. This is expressly made clear in *The Worth-Ship Mandate,* with series of scriptural details to support the various elucidations Lady Rebecca outlines in its pages.

I love the overview of the Old Testament tabernacle, done in chapter 5 (a more detailed work follows soon). Here, Lady Rebecca elaborates how Christ forms the center and core of the Tabernacle even before His manifestation in the New Testament - to prove His indispensability in the whole practice of worship.

Take a little of your time to go through this amazing revelation of worship, neatly packaged to perfection too. Order a copy to bless a loved one.

The Worth-Ship Mandate is a real textbook for churches and worshipers. It is designed to inspire you to worship, and I highly recommended it.

Rev Dickson Tuffour Sarpong
Head Pastor, ICGC Jesus Temple
Koforidua E/R Ghana

REVIEWS

The Worth-Ship Mandate is deep in revelation. It provides great enlightenment to the Body of Christ regarding the nature of true worship. Indeed, a true worshiper must first be saved and rooted in the Word which is Jesus… and I agree with Lady Becky.

Jojo Immanuel-Lawson
Worship Leader, Music Evangelist

Pastor Becky's depth of insight into the subject of worship, both as a worship leader and a teacher of the Word, makes it an easy, yet impactful read. This book is definitely a powerful tool and catalyst for spiritual revival.

Isabella Ogo Uzodike
Worship Leader, Singer & Song Writer

What is contained in this book is unique; especially, the part that draws a distinction between what is and what is NOT worship. *The Worth-Ship Mandate* is full of divinely-inspired revelations, geared towards making every reader a better worshipper. Get a copy for your-self; it is a perfect gift for a loved one too.

Rev Isaac Osei-Edwards
Child Evangelist and Trainer
Pastor-in-charge, ICGC Potter's Temple, South London

"God is a spirit and they that worship Him must worship Him in spirit and in truth."
(John 4:24)

PREAMBLE

Dear reader, manifold blessings to you in the name of The Father, Son and Holy Spirit. You are welcome on board this journey of discovering the Father's own design and plan for the ACT and ART of WORSHIP. This book is a result of a lifelong search; a quest that stems from my passion to touch the Father's heart and my longing desire to live a 'worshipful' life as a believer.

This school of worship, which spans nearly three decades of my Christian life, has been an incredible one with a lot learned and a lot to share! Some of the topics were directly inspired by the Holy Spirit as I kept searching for answers about WORSHIP; others were as result of experiences I had as I discharged ministry duties as a worship leader, teacher or speaker.

A key lesson I learnt growing up in the Lord is that, worship (Greek: *Proskuneo,* pronounced as *pros-koo-neh'-o* and interpreted as prostrating oneself in homage to a higher being), is a **life that is lived (an attitude) and not just a mere act we perform on stage!**

May the Lord grant us all the revelation needed to see the light on this journey.

INTRODUCTION

Worship is *Worth-Ship!* Worship is love, even romantic love, comparable to the relationship (union) between a husband and his wife! Paul describes it as a mystery.

> [31]For this reason a man will leave his father and mother and be united to his wife, and the two will become one flesh.
>
> [32]This mystery is profound, but I am speaking about Christ and the church.
>
> **Ephesians 5:31,32**

True, spiritual worship stems from a relationship (union), like marriage. It is a free flow of gratitude from the soul in response to God, first and foremost, for who He is, and secondly, for choosing (marrying) us into His kingdom.

We should not be coerced by worship leaders, instruments, etc into worship. We must worship out of *this* revelation, which goes beyond our emotions and feelings; how happy or sad we are; how pleased or satisfied or disappointed we are or what God has or has not done for!

The subject of *worship* is at the heart of the Father's business and undoubtedly, no true child of God can excel in their journey without being 'worshipful' or 'praiseful'.

Jesus sets us all examples. As we can see from the prayer that He taught his disciples, worship is a priority. It tops the prayer list that Jesus taught in the Lord's Prayer:

> This, then, is how you should pray: "Our Father in heaven, hallowed be your name..."
>
> **Matthew 6:9 NIV**

Acknowledging our Father; sanctifying, blessing and honouring His name (out of our love for Him) is the first step in gaining access to His heart. Before laying our petitions before Him, our worship must go up. Beloved, our worship, sacrifices, praise and thankfulness are the steps that grant us the ticket to His presence, and once we gain that access we become His delight and He makes "all other things" follow us. *In effect, your worship creates the atmosphere for God to attend to you and your needs.*

There are a lot of hidden treasures in this aspect of our walk as Christians. Come with me as we search some deep places in the Bible to gain understanding of the concept of this mystery called *worship.*

It is my prayer that by the end of this book, we will all be changed into His own image and the eyes of our understanding will be enlightened to become good Spirit-and-truth worshippers that the Father is searching for.

Welcome on board **FLIGHT J 4:24!**

CHAPTER ONE

WORSHIP: WHAT IT IS & WHAT IT'S NOT

We sometimes pray it, sing it, rehearse it, perform it and even package it for sale. Many engage in responsive readings, ceremonies and rituals. Others dance around, lift their hands and shout. Some speak in tongues and perform dramatic acts until they run out of energy. Still, there are those who sit quietly and meditate their prayers or just bow in solitude and listen in. But are these acts what worship is all about?

Before we proceed, let us establish a few truths about Worship.

SEVEN THINGS THAT WORSHIP IS NOT

1. Worship is not concert or a gig.
2. Worship is not drama or a performance on stage.
3. Worship is not only an act.
4. Worship is not an item to be ticked on the church's agenda during meetings.
5. Worship is not just about music.
6. Worship is not a moment to excite ourselves or simply get our congregations excited "before God."
7. Worship is not what we do to "wait for the preacher to arrive."

SEVEN THINGS THAT DEFINE TRUE WORSHIP

1. True worship is Spiritual.
2. True worship is scarce, rare, uncommon.
3. True worship is LIVED; it is a lifestyle.
4. True worship is lived from the inside out.
5. True worship is an upshot of a love relationship between the worshipper and the Father (like that of a husband and his wife).

6. True worship is done out of revelation.
7. True worshippers are continually sought after by the Father.

INSIGHT FROM JESUS

Jesus gave us an insight into what true worship is when he spoke to the woman at the well.

> [23]But the hour cometh, and now is, when the true worshippers shall worship the Father in spirit and in truth: for the Father seeketh such to worship him.
>
> [24]God is a Spirit: and they that worship him must worship him in spirit and in truth.
>
> **John 4:23-24**

From this scripture, we can infer that there are two types of worship: *true* and *false* worship. As pursuers of TRUE worship, let us consider what Jesus prescribed in this scripture:

1. True worship is spiritual.
2. True worship is done in Truth (honesty).
3. The Father seeks true worshippers.

DEFINITIONS OF WORSHIP

According to the Webster's Dictionary, the term ***worship*** means *to regard (something or somebody) with great or extravagant respect, honour, or devotion.*

The Cambridge Dictionary makes it even clearer: *to have or show a strong feeling of respect and admiration for God or a god.*

Words that are synonymous with *worship* include: adoration, deference, glorification, reverence, veneration, idealisation, affection, fancy, favour, fondness, liking, love, appreciation, esteem, regard and respect.

From these definitions, we get the picture of a "lesser being" who chooses by his or her own accord to show respect, humility, holy fear, reverence and commitment to a "higher being" (in our case, God).

We can also infer that during the process of worship, one party must assume the "lower" position in order to submit, commit, respect and demonstrate reverence to the "higher" being. This "higher" being is called *deity* in some reference books. You will agree with me that this vouchsafing of reverence, devotion and respect to something is a trait imbedded in humans, practised by all as part of our nature and make-up. Yes, all humans gravitate towards a higher power to submit to in worship.

The truth is, worship is a virtue inherent in every human. We were all born with the desire to worship something. No human being is fulfilled or content without the act of worship.

EVERYONE WORSHIPS SOMETHING

Even non-believers such as atheists Agnostics, Antitheists, Sceptics, Pantheists and Humanists all do offer some form of worship. The difference lies in what a person believes in and focuses on. Consider a description of the categories of people:

Atheists: people who do not believe in the existence of God or gods.

Agnostics: people who believe there is a God who is and will forever be unknown to man. (Weak agnostics believe that the mystery of God's existence might be uncovered in the future).

Antitheists: these believe that religion is dangerous and harmful.

Sceptics: They question every aspect of religiosity, rituals or devotion to a deity. (I think there are a lot of sceptics in the church!).

Humanists: They believe in being spiritual, but their spirituality is achieved through actions or works. Humanists are ethical, principled and decent people, but these are not synonymous with being saved because we are not saved through works.

Pantheists: these believe that God exists all around us, but not in one manifestation or form.

All the above non-believers, as well as those on the other side of the spectrum, including Hindus, Muslims, Sikhs, Buddhists, Judaists and those of the Baha'i Faith, perform some form of worship. How one differs from the other is determined by WHAT each believes in, respects or worships.

For instance, in order to feed his natural desire for worship, an atheist may place his faith in and worship his riches, wealth, pride, qualifications, achievements, relationships, connections, etc. Those who do not identify with any of the aforementioned, may simply rely on drinking, drugging or other social practices to satisfy the natural instinct for worship. These items, states or phenomena, could become a person's FOCUS or OBJECT of worship!

We all know of renowned and celebrated showbiz personalities who became idols that fans worship. I was not a follower of Michael Jackson, but for curiosity sake, I watched one clip that featured the crowd literally fainting in admiration for him! Some were bursting out in tears, kneeling, jumping the stage to hug him, leaning forward to get a feel of him or perform some sort of homage for their star. This was their way of expressing worship - obviously to a mortal man!

I have also witnessed countless moments during cooperate church worship sessions where believers have fallen prostrate, cried or shouted unto the Lord in the process. Yes, This is the power of worship!

#Lesson: *Everybody is a slave to something – the object of their worship! What are you a slave to?*

WORSHIP IS WORTH-SHIP!

Word Study: Worth-Ship

The following is an etymology of my coined compound word, WORTH-SHIP.

Worth is an old Germanic word, defined in the

Merriam Webster's dictionary as *value, wealth* or *riches*. Synonyms associated with the word *worth* include: cost, price, weight, dignity, importance, rate, usefulness, significance and quality.

Ship: has dual meanings, both of which are relevant to the purpose of our study. First, it is used as a suffix added to root words to denote condition, character, office, skill, etc. (for example, clerkship, friendship, statesmanship). Secondly, the word *ship* is a noun that describes a vessel used for travelling on sea.

The word *worship* itself stems from the old English *weorscipe,* which is interpreted as *worthiness* or *acknowledgment of worth to something or somebody*. Indeed, we give things attention based on how much *worth,* value or price we place on them, which is all based on our revealed perspective of them. Worship is indeed WORTH-SHIP!

True worship is the outflow of an inner revelation that leads the worshipper to showcase the worthiness of what he/she worships. How worthy is God to you?

LESSONS FROM THE ALABASTER BOX

The Bible records two distinct stories of *The Woman with The Alabaster Box*. Matthew, Mark and John refer to one incident in Bethany, where a nameless lady, named in John's gospel as Mary of Bethany, did something extraordinary. Jesus had gathered at table with some known pundits of the town, including Lazarus whom he had raised from the dead. Although Mary would not have been allowed to enter a gathering of men, especially "men who matter," Pharisees and teachers of the law, she ignored the limitations of culture and tradition, and did something spectacular. Her action touched Jesus and prompted him to prophesy that her name would be mentioned everywhere the gospel is preached. To date, this simple lady remains significant in the annals of scripture.

What did she do? John and Mark recorded it in the following texts.

> [1]Then Jesus six days before the passover came to Bethany, where Lazarus was, which had been dead, whom he raised from the dead.
>
> [2]There they made him a supper; and Martha served: but Lazarus was one of them that sat at the table with him.
>
> [3]Then took Mary a pound of ointment of spikenard, very costly, and anointed the feet of Jesus, and wiped his feet with her

hair: and the house was filled with the odour of the ointment.

[4]Then saith one of his disciples, Judas Iscariot, Simon's son, which should betray him,

[5]Why was not this ointment sold for three hundred pence, and given to the poor?

[6]This he said, not that he cared for the poor; but because he was a thief, and had the bag, and bare what was put therein.

[7]Then said Jesus, Let her alone: against the day of my burying hath she kept this.

[8]For the poor always ye have with you; but me ye have not always.

John 12:1-8

[3]And being in Bethany in the house of Simon the leper, as he sat at meat, there came a woman having an alabaster box of ointment of spikenard very precious; and she brake the box, and poured it on his head.

[4]And there were some that had indignation within themselves, and said, why was this waste of the ointment made?

[5]For it might have been sold for more than three hundred pence and have been given to the poor. And they murmured against her.

[6]And Jesus said, let her alone; why trouble ye her? she hath wrought a good work on me.

[7]For ye have the poor with you always, and whensoever ye will ye may do them good: but me ye have not always.

[8]She hath done what she could: she is come aforehand to anoint my body to the burying.

[9]Verily I say unto you, wheresoever this gospel shall be preached throughout the whole world, this also that she hath done shall be spoken of for a memorial of her.

Mark 14:3-9

A number of things caught my attention from these passages above. As previously noted, the woman broke all protocols of the day, including the culture and traditions of men. Jesus was sitting with men for dinner in an era when women were not expected to be around, let alone 'bump' into the gathering and do her own thing.

In addition to the above, the following are worthy of note:

- The ointment that the woman poured on Jesus was expensive; it was valued at a year's wages.
- She did not delicately empty the oil on Jesus; instead, she broke the alabaster box. This meant that it was not possible to put its pieces together again.
- She poured ALL of the ointment on Jesus.

Luke recorded a slightly different episode which has led researchers to suggest it is a separate incident from the other account. What matters more for the purpose of our study is the common reference to an expensive bottle of perfume. We will discuss the relevance of this after reading Luke's account:

> [37]And, behold, a woman in the city, which was a sinner, when she knew that Jesus sat at meat in the Pharisee's house, brought an alabaster box of ointment,
>
> [38]And stood at his feet behind him weeping, and began to wash his feet with tears, and did wipe them with the hairs of her head, and kissed his feet, and anointed them with the ointment.

> [44]And he turned to the woman, and said unto Simon, Seest thou this woman? I entered into thine house, thou gavest me no water for my feet: but she hath washed my feet with tears, and wiped them with the hairs of her head.
>
> [45]Thou gavest me no kiss: but this woman since the time I came in hath not ceased to kiss my feet.
>
> [47]Wherefore I say unto thee, Her sins, which are many, are forgiven; for she loved much: but to whom little is forgiven, the same loveth little.
>
> **Luke 7:37,38,44,45,47**

This account took place around Galilee in the house of Simon the Pharisee, about a year before the crucifixion (Luke 7:1,11). The nameless woman was forgiven of many sins and she came to show her deep appreciation by anointing the feet of Jesus with her tears and ointment from her alabaster box.

The focus of our study is on the presence of an alabaster box of precious perfume and the concept of *Worth-Ship* presented in both narratives.

THE ALABASTER BOX

Alabaster was a stone commonly found in Israel. It was a hard material that resembled white marble and is referred to as one of the precious stones used in the decoration of Solomon's Temple (1 Chronicles 29:2). In Song of Songs, the beloved man is described as having legs like "alabaster columns" (ESV) or "pillars of marble" (NIV, KJV). We cannot overemphasise the priceless nature of this alabaster container.

Considering the solid nature of the alabaster box, we need to wonder how much effort the women put into BREAKING it in order to release the expensive perfume it contained. Think about it: we are talking about a stone here and for a woman to be able to break it open, she must have applied a great deal of energy, passion and time. But she did it!

NO ORDINARY OIL

Refering to the oil, the word *spikenard* is used in the King James Version. Other translations simply say "pure nard." Spikenard is a costly perfumed ointment much valued in ancient times. It had a strong, distinctive aroma, similar to an essential oil. It also clinged to the skin and hair and continued to release its intoxicating fragrance. It was also thought to have medicinal properties. One feature that set spikenard apart from other ointments is the many hairy spikes shooting out from one root.

The uniqueness of this fragrance and its aroma indicated that the women had offered their very best. In fact, those who witnessed this act of worship estimated the value of the contents poured on Jesus' feet to be equivalent to a year's wages. Yes, the perfume was expensive! When Mary broke open her alabaster box, "the house was filled with the fragrance of the perfume" (John 12:3).

There is no gainsaying that Mary perceived something that other people did not see. She had a revelation of the *worth* of Christ's love for her, and this moved her to dispose of her possession, even to the equivalent of a year's wages!

WHAT IS YOUR ALABASTER?

Anything we give attention to in life; whatever we accord deep respect, honour or devotion to, becomes the object and entity of our worship. In real terms, this could be anything from self (physical make-up, ego), to family, friends, career, titles, possessions or anything that gives us pleasure. Let us briefly explore a few.

Career

Some people live for their careers. They are preoccupied with work, and whatever they spend their time on has to be work-related. For others, it is their family. They will move heaven and earth to make their wife, husband, child, mom or dad feel comfortable. Some parents would do anything to give their children all the pleasures a child could have - good education, holidays, fun clubs and anything they desire. The parents feel fulfilled as fathers, mothers or guardians when they give such services or sacrifices to their children.

Physical appearance

There are those who spend a considerable amount of time working on their looks. They spend a lot on clothes, shoes, making-up and other things that make them feel like "real" humans! There is nothing wrong with these things; however, the question remains: have we made gods out of them? It displeases the Father when our commitments and dedications take *His* place in our lives.

Titles

There is nothing fundamentally wrong with titles. I love the fact that I have achieved some academic feats in my life so far - all glory to God! Nevertheless, titles should never stand in the way of or compete with God in my life. Sadly, some people derive their sense of worth from their titles. Indirectly, they say to God: "Excuse me, I hold a PhD/MPHIL/LLB holder; I am a government official and a diplomat. Why should I bow or kneel down in worship?" Only pride and self-centeredness will make a person think in this way.

How pleasantly humbling it is to see some renowned spiritual fathers such us Rev. Dr. Mensa Otabil (who chooses to be called Pastor), of the *International Central Gospel Churches* (ICGC), and Rev. Enoch Adeboye (affectionately called Daddy G.O.), of the *Redeemed Christian Churches,* kneel during congregational worship sessions! They send a very positive signal to the heavens and their followers that regardless of popularity and success in ministry, we should submit to the Lord who has called us.

Now, try answering the question again: *What is your Alabaster Box?*

CHAPTER TWO

THE ULTIMATE ENTITY & FOCUS OF WORSHIP

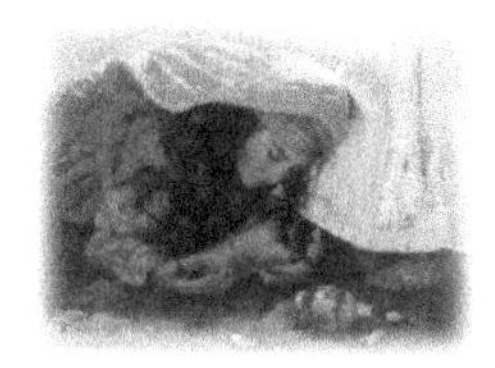

The ultimate and perfect entity and focus of our worship as Christians should be God to whom we belong - our Maker, Saviour, Shepherd and Lover. We were made for His glory. In fact, the Lord Himself seeks for those who acknowledge and relate to Him as such in their worship. He is looking for *true worshippers* (John 4:24).

THE LORD OUR MAKER

We must worship God from the perspective of a "Manufacturer and a product."

> Even every one that is called by my name: for I have created him for my glory, I have formed him; yea, I have made him.
>
> **Isaiah 43:7**

> Thou art worthy O Lord, to receive glory and honour and power: for thou hast created all things, and for thy pleasure they are and were created.
>
> **Revelation 4:11**

> Know that the LORD, He is God; It is He who has made us, and not we ourselves.
>
> **Psalm 100:3**

When you purchase a gadget or an appliance, your first instinct is to look for the manufacturer's instruction manual on how to use it. Why do we do this? Simply because the maker of the product is most qualified to explain how to operate the product. Without referring to that little piece of paper, it may be difficult—impossible in some cases—to operate or use the appliance. As well, it is comforting to know that when you have a problem with any gadget, you can consult or contact the manufacturer of the item for a resolution of the issue.

I once had a problem with my Samsung S7

smart phone. It went berserk and I thought I had lost some precious photos and videos! When I contacted Samsung, they booked me in for a remote tutorial to try and find the images. I knew that only the original manufacturers could solve the problem I had with my phone. If, for any reason, they could not resolve it, then no other company would be able to fix it! Why? Because no other authority can surpass that of the original manufacturer in providing a solution to its product!

In the same way, there is no better place to abide than in the presence of my Maker. The psalmist said, *It is He who has made us, and not we ourselves.* We must "report" to our Maker regularly and consistently. By reporting, I mean showing yourself to Him daily and merely saying, "Dear Lord, here I am."

"...Here I am to worship

Here I am to bow down

Here I am say that you're my God

Altogether lovely

Altogether worthy

Altogether wonderful to me![1]

> ...the sons of God came to present themselves before the LORD...
>
> **Job 1:6a**

Now, this "presentation" by "the sons of God" was not a one-off occurrence; it was a regular practice. If you are a child of God, it is imperative that you regularly present (report) yourself before Him in worship. It is your way of surrendering to His authority and lordship over your life. Worship is the process through which we connect with our maker and tap strength and grace to face each day. May the Lord be our Helper, that we may uphold the attitude and culture of worship! Yes, worship is our mode and method of staying in tune with our God, even our Maker!

> ***#Lesson:** A worship-less Christian is a powerless out of tune disconnected or disconnecting Christian!*

THE LORD, OUR SHEPHERD

We must worship God with the understanding that He is our Shepherd and we are His sheep—the sheep of *His pasture* (meaning that our source, our feeding ground belongs to Him).

> We are His people and the sheep of His pasture.
>
> **Psalm 100:3b**

Psalm 23 is, by far, the most popular Psalm. It brings a lot of comfort to believers as it stipulates a range of benefits that the shepherd lavishes on the sheep. However, we must not lose sight of the scenario created in the opening verse. For the sake of this study, let us go through the whole psalm so we can unpack the benefits therein.

> [1]The Lord is my shepherd; I shall not want.
>
> [2]He makes me to lie down in green pastures; He leads me beside the still waters.
>
> [3]He restores my soul; He leads me in the paths of righteousness for His name's sake.
>
> [4]Yea, though I walk through the valley of the shadow of death, I will fear no evil; for You are with me; Your rod and Your staff, they comfort me.
>
> [5]You prepare a table before me in the presence of my enemies; You anoint my head with oil; My cup runs over.

[6]Surely goodness and mercy shall follow me all the days of my life; And I will dwell in the house of the Lord, Forever.

Psalm 23:1-6

There are eleven benefits we can deduce from this Psalm, as follows:

1. ***Green Pastures:*** abundance, provision etc.
2. ***Still waters:*** symbolising peace.
3. ***Restoration:*** Through Christ, we are reinstated into the original status and adopted as children of God.
4. ***Righteousness:*** He helps us to live right
5. ***No fear of evil:*** because He will conquer evil on our behalf.
6. ***Comfort:*** God grants us our well-being and sanity.
7. ***Sets a table before me:*** Promotion in the presence of opposition.
8. ***Anointing:*** Empowerment for productivity.
9. ***Cup runs over:*** Overflowing grace.
10. ***Goodness and mercies:*** What we work for and the kindness we do not deserve (mercy) become ours for a lifetime.

11. ***I will dwell in the house of the Lord forever:*** The consequence of a totally-surrendered life in worship is dwelling with, connecting with and living for God forever.

Now watch this: Both the opening verse in this psalm: *'The Lord is **my Shepherd**'* and the closing line: *"...and I will **dwell in the house forever**"* have something in common. They both talk about connection, relationship and having a kind of rapport with the Lord. It is as if the Lord is saying, "I desire to load you with benefits, shower you with favour and bless you on all sides. However, you must understand that the extent of your surrender to, connection with and relationship with Me, the Lord, as a sheep to its shepherd, will determine the extent of your access to the list of benefits thereof!"

Once this connection is secured, that 'sheep' would not struggle to abide in the house (in the presence) of the Lord because it has become a delight and a pleasure rather than a revulsive and contemptible obligation.

The first verse of this popular psalm is the condition upon which the entire list of benefits depend. In other words, if verse one is negated (if the Lord is *not* my shepherd), there is no guarantee that we can receive any of the eleven benefits listed from the second verse downwards. No wonder it starts with the statement, "The Lord is *my* shepherd,' which makes it personal too!

The psalmist is very sure of safety, provision and protection from his Shepherd, and could therefore say, *"I shall not want" anything else.* That is, *I shall not be in need of any good thing in life.* This declaration was borne out of a personal revelation he had about his relationship with his Lord.

David used the shepherd-and-sheep metaphor to depict his own relationship with God. This description stems from his own experience as a shepherd, looking after his father's sheep in the wilderness. The bible records how he protected his father's sheep from preying animals and tended the ewes and lambs before the Lord called him (Psalm 78:70-71). His experience as a shepherd gave him a personal understanding of the kind of relationship that God desires to have with His people. David knew by experience the care and tender affection of a good shepherd has for his flock. He understood what the sheep needed from a shepherd, and how comforting it was to them to have a skilful and faithful shepherd.

God is not just a shepherd; He is a GOOD one! Jesus confidently made this reference about Himself.

> I am the good shepherd: the good shepherd giveth his life for the sheep.
>
> **John 10:11**

Our Shepherd does not sleep or slumber. He goes all out to protect, guide and provide for His flock (the Church), even to the extent of dying for His own. Therefore, Christ qualifies himself with the adjective 'GOOD'.

#Lesson: *If the Lord is our shepherd, then we should be like sheep unto Him.*

A sheep is obedient, harmless, meek and mild, useful and silent before the butcher too! Oh yes - even to the point of death (of any kind). We must be willing to surrender to our shepherd. Sometimes, we are so excited with God until He begins to prune us or, as it were, put certain things in us to death! That is when the test of whether we are sheep or goats becomes obvious! Do we still say, "your will be done" when the Lord prunes us or do we challenge, question or even rebel against God?

Being the Lord's sheep means we will enjoy provision, protection and care from Him, as well as chastising, correction and the ocassional slaughter-house experience, which forms a part of our worship of Him.

If David penned this psalm before his coming to the crown, then we must understand what moved him to say that he "shall not want." He trusted in God alone! This is because we know that David went through a lot of hard times, including near-death experiences with his adversaries, Saul being the chief of them.

Why, then, did David declare that he shall not want? Perhaps, he implied that if God was his shepherd, he is assured that he would not lack anything he needed; whenever a need arose, he would be aptly supplied. It also meant that if he did not have anything he desired, it may be a case of it not being fitting or good for him at the time—we should, likewise, have the same perception. Evidently, from what we know of David's life, this understanding helped him to develop the habit of patience and humility, and kept him trusting in God.

May the Lord help us all to strive towards being the sheep of His pasture, worshiping and being loyal to Him so we can partake in all the benefits that follow.

THE LORD, OUR SAVIOUR

We need to worship God from the perspective of a wretched, dying soul, saved by a loving Saviour. We were the doomed and condemned souls and He is the wonderful Saviour who delivered us from destruction! We must consciously keep this idea fresh in our hearts because it keeps us humble before God.

> But thou shalt remember that thou wast a bondman (slave) in Egypt, and the LORD thy God redeemed thee thence.
>
> **Deuteronomy 15:15**

We were once slaves in the hands of a wicked Pharaoh in Egypt. Egypt refers to the world that is controlled by the devil. Just as Pharaoh and his men put Israel to hellish slave duties, using them to build numerous projects for himself without any reward, so were we bonded by the prince of this world to do all sorts of evil deeds that destroyed our bodies and destinies. Israel remained in bondage until Moses emerged as their deliverer. Likewise, we were in captivity until Jesus came to rescue us from the bondage of sin!

Let us remember, therefore, where we were, in the dungeon of sin with its subsequent reproach. Let us also remember how merciful the Father was to send His ONLY BEGOTTEN SON to redeem us unto newness. This should inspire us daily to worship without any reservation, but rather, in appreciation to Him. He saved us. He redeemed us. He restored us unto Himself.

This old testament scripture is replicated in the epistle of Paul to the Ephesians.

> [1]As for you, you were dead in your transgressions and sins,
>
> [2]in which you used to live when you followed the ways of this world and of the ruler of the kingdom of the air, the spirit who is now at work in those who are disobedient.
>
> [3]All of us also lived among them at one time, gratifying the cravings of our flesh and following its desires and thoughts. Like the rest, we were by nature deserving of wrath.
>
> [4]But because of his great love for us, God, who is rich in mercy,
>
> [5]made us alive with Christ even when we were dead in transgressions—it is by grace you have been saved.
>
> **Ephesians 2:1-5**

You unravel me, with a melody
You surround me with a song
Of deliverance, from my enemies
Till all my fears are gone

Chorus

I'm no longer a slave to fear
I am a child of God
I'm no longer a slave to fear
I am a child of God

From my mother's womb
You have chosen me
Love has called my name
I've been born again, into a family
Your blood flows through my veins

I am surrounded
By the arms of the father
I am surrounded
By songs of deliverance
We've been liberated
From our bondage
We're the sons and the daughters
Let us sing our freedom

You split the sea
So I could walk right through it
My fears were drowned in perfect love
You rescued me
And I will stand and sing
I am the child of God
You split the sea

So I could walk right through it
You drowned my fears in perfect love
You rescued me
And I will stand and sing
I am the child of God (yes I am)[2]

This song, a fresh expression of worship by the American group, Bethel Music, is a perfect song of deliverance. Here, the song writer speaks of Christ's redeeming power that has rescued him from the bondage of sin *"so I will stand and sing..."* Yes, we have been rescued for one purpose only – to stand and sing his praises!

> Who redeemeth thy life from destruction; who crowneth thee with lovingkindness and tender mercies
>
> **Psalm 103:4**

Word study: Redeem

The Hebrew word translated into the verb 'redeem' in this scripture is *gaal* [l;a"G]. It is a legal term for the deliverance or buying back of a person, a right or freedom which they had previously but had lost (e.g. through debt). *Goel,* the participle of *gaal* [l;a"G], is the term for the person who performed the duties of a *redeemer.*

From this scripture, we know that Christ did not only rescue us from doom, but also "crowned" us "with lovingkindness and tender mercies." This means that God has paid a price to bring us back to where we began - in the glorious atmosphere of Eden. And He seeks to treat us with consideration, gentleness, warmth and affection.

Hesed, the Hebrew word for "loving-kindness," relates to God's loyalty to Himself and His creation; He does not wait for our self-improvement efforts before He loves us. Yahweh is forgiving (even when we miss it again), compassionate, gracious, lenient, for-bearing and humane in His dealings with us. Oh, what a Saviour!

> [8]God is all mercy and grace—not quick to anger, is rich in love.
>
> [9]God is good to one and all; everything he does is suffused (bathed/saturated/ covered) with grace.
>
> **Psalm 145:8-9 MSG**

Whatever He does is powered by GRACE! GRACE is a metaphor for Christ!

> Who hath delivered us from the power of darkness, and hath translated us into the kingdom of his dear Son: In whom we have redemption through his blood, even the forgiveness of sins.
>
> **Colossians 1:13-14**

The precious price was His Son, Jesus! That is to say, He paid the price for our sins with His own self! No power of death or sin can tie us down, as long as we continue to plug into Him - the vine. In him *"we have redemption through his blood - even the forgiveness of sins."* But remember, He did all that for one main reason – so we can "stand and sing" His song!

THE LORD, OUR LOVER

After saving us, the Lord seeks our heart. He desires a love relationship with us, the kind of love that is comparable to that of a married man and wife. The description of a marriage relation as a figure of speech to compare believers' relationship with God is very frequent in scripture. Recall that we looked briefly at a new testament reference in Ephesians 5:31-32. Now let us explore what the old testament says about this perspective of our relationship with God.

[8]Now when I passed by thee, and looked upon thee, behold, thy time was the time of love; and I spread my skirt over thee, and covered thy nakedness: yea, I sware unto thee, and entered into a covenant with thee, saith the Lord GOD, and thou becamest mine.

[9]Then washed I thee with water; yea, I thoroughly washed away thy blood from thee, and I anointed thee with oil.

[10]I clothed thee also with broidered work, and shod thee with badgers' skin, and I girded thee about with fine linen, and I covered thee with silk.

[11]I decked thee also with ornaments, and I put bracelets upon thy hands, and a chain on thy neck.

[12]And I put a jewel on thy forehead, and earrings in thine ears, and a beautiful crown upon thine head.

[13]Thus wast thou decked with gold and silver; and thy raiment was of fine linen, and silk, and broidered work; thou didst eat fine flour, and honey, and oil: and thou wast exceeding beautiful, and thou didst prosper into a kingdom.

> [14]And thy renown went forth among the heathen for thy beauty: for it was perfect through my comeliness, which I had put upon thee, saith the Lord GOD.
>
> **Ezekiel 16:8-14**

In the first seven verses of this prophetic poetic chapter of Ezekiel, the prophet lists a range of infant initiation rites practised in the eastern culture to reflect how Yahweh's relationship with Israel had developed. Israel, like an unfortunate, vulnerable child, lacked certain privileges, handlings and procedures, such as rubbing in salt, cutting of the navel and the overall care needed for the proper growth of a child. God depicted a vivid description to show the humble and poor beginnings of Israel, originally from Canaan, a land filled with moral decadence. The prophetic poem revealed that *"On the day [Israel] were born,"* with no one to care for her, but rather *"loathed"*and *"thrown out into the open field,"* and left to struggle to death *"in [her] own blood,"* as practised by some worldly people, who abandon their disabled children at river sides and open fields to be literally devoured by wild beasts; *"the Lord passed by and said 'live'!"* Oh how sweet it feels to know the privilege of being called into His kingdom!

> [6]And when I passed by you and saw you struggling in your own blood, I said to you in your blood, 'Live!' Yes, I said to you in your blood, 'Live!'
>
> [7]I made you thrive like a plant in the field; and you grew, matured, and became very beautiful. Your breasts were formed, your hair grew, but you were naked and bare.
>
> **Ezekiel 16:6-7**

When our adversaries wished our death, God said, "live". He brought life to us and made us thrive like a plant in the field.

Hear this: after rescuing you from your struggles and raising you into a 'beautiful' woman, God then decided to cover your nakedness and marry you to seal you as His possession! The prophet described Israel as a *vulnerable woman* whose time of misery and affliction was *met with love and protection from a rescuing suitor* (husband) who covered her nakedness (*"spread my skirt over thee…"*) and entered into a covenant with her that made her HIS bride.

This was in reference to mount Sinai, when the covenant between God and Israel was sealed and ratified. Those to whom God gives spiritual life, He takes into covenant with Himself. By this covenant, they became His own -

His subjects and servants who do not only owe Him a duty, but also benefit from His treasure and privileges. You are the new Israel; worship him with revelation!

The "washing, anointing, clothing with embroidered work, jewellery on forehead and sandals" were all part of the marriage rites performed for virgins. As the new and spiritual Israel, we see how precious we are in God's sight; knowing that God does not only save and cover us, He also loads us with riches and spoils us, like the bride of a rich king, with superfluities, wealth and felicities.

Oh, what a priceless salvation! Our worship of God should flow from this insight. We worship Him as our highly esteemed husband to whom we are privileged to be married! If you are born again, you are His bride and He is your valued, revered groom. He covered your weaknesses and nakedness, and covenanted with you to be his own. What a privilege! This bond of love between you and God must stimulate your worship of Him.

Wonderful, merciful Savior
Precious Redeemer and Friend
Who would have thought that a Lamb
Could rescue the souls of men
Oh, You rescue the souls of men

Counselor, Comforter, Keeper
Spirit we long to embrace
You offer hope when our hearts have
Hopelessly lost our way
Oh, we've hopelessly lost the way

You are the One that we praise
You are the One we adore
You give the healing and grace
Our hearts always hunger for
Oh, our hearts always hunger for

Almighty, infinite Father
Faithfully loving Your own
Here in our weakness You find us
Falling before Your throne
Oh, we're falling before Your throne

You are the One that we praise
You are the One we adore
You give the healing and grace
Our hearts always hunger for
Oh, our hearts always hunger for[3]

A CALL FROM HIS HEART!

Dear reader, *true and pure worship begins with relationship*. There are no two ways about it. A pure relationship with God as your Maker, Saviour, Shepherd or Lover requires the simple step of believing and receiving:

Believe in the Lord Jesus Christ as the lamb that was sacrificed to reconcile man back to God.

Accept Jesus Christ as your Lord and personal Saviour.

Confess with your mouth, what you have believed and accepted.

> For whosoever shall call upon the name of the Lord shall be saved.
>
> **Romans 10:13**

> They said, "Put your trust (believe) in the Lord Jesus Christ and you and your family will be saved from the punishment of sin."
>
> **Acts 16:31 NLV**

Please note: sin will certainly be punished!

> For the wages of sin is death…
>
> **Romans 6:23a NIV**

Sin leads to eternal death, which is worse than physical death. Eternal death is a state of spiritual separation from God, lasting for all eternity. People who are spiritually dead will end up in Hell, a place of torment and anguish.

What is sin? Sin, mentioned many times in the Bible, is defined in the original translations as "to miss the mark." The "mark" is the standard of righteousness - what is right, good, and acceptable - set by God from the beginning of creation, and displayed to us through Christ Jesus. Therefore, we have all missed the mark, right from birth. That is why the bible says, *"For all have sinned and fall short of the glory of God"* (Romans 3:23).

As a result of being born with a sin nature, inherited from our foreparents, Adam and Eve, all of us were born separated from God and in need of a way back into the glory that was lost.

Jesus Christ, the Son of God, came down to earth, and died a painful death on the cross to save and redeem us. By His death, He paid the full price for our redemption.

Jesus did not only die, He rose again after three days, and it is through faith in Him that we are saved.

> [16]For God so loved the world, that He gave His only begotten Son, that whoever believes in Him shall not perish, but have eternal life.
>
> [17]For God did not send His Son into the world to condemn the world, but to save the world through Him.
>
> **John 3:16-17**

Jesus Christ, our cornerstone, came as God in the form of The Son, to reconcile man back to Himself after the fall of man in Eden.

> Behold! The Lamb of God who takes away the sin of the world!
>
> **John 1:29b**

Please note: it is not by works, lest none of us would qualify, but by believing in Christ as the WAY to reconcile with the Father. Therefore, the 'sin' (in singular) of the world mentioned in this scripture is referring to the sin of rebellion – the refusal to acknowledge Jesus as Lord of lords!

You see, acknowledging His lordship is your first step to relating with Him, which is really what worship is about! It is not necessarily about the wrong things you have done to yourself or mankind but more to do with your surrender to Him as your Lord. For in surrendering to Him, he gives you the grace to overcome evil or wrongdoing, which is an act of rebellion against God's authority.

Please pray the prayer below if you have not done so meaningfully, but now are convicted by the reading so far. (Every true believer, including myself, has said this prayer at least once before beginning a walk with the Lord).

Remember that it is not merely the words in the prayer that saves, but your faith, conviction, repentance and God's own power.

SALVATION PRAYER

Lord Jesus, for too long I have lived life my own way. But now, I am convicted. I know that I am a sinner and that I cannot save myself. No longer will I close the door when I hear you knocking. By faith, I gratefully receive your gift of salvation. I am ready to trust you as my Lord and Saviour. I believe you are the Son of God who died on the cross for my sins and rose from the dead on the third day. Thank you for bearing my sins and giving me the gift of eternal life. I believe your words are true. Come into my heart, Lord Jesus, and be my Saviour and write my name in the book of Life; that I may inherit the beautiful place you are preparing for all who believe in you. Amen.

If you prayed this prayer, then my friend, according to God's word, you are saved and have been made part of God's own family! Hallelujah!

> [9]That if thou shalt confess with thy mouth the Lord Jesus, and shalt believe in thine heart that God hath raised him from the dead, thou shalt be saved.
>
> [10]For with the heart man believeth unto righteousness; and with the mouth confession is made unto salvation.
>
> **Romans 10:9-10**

---

1. *Here I am to worship,* Lyrics by Tim Hughes

2. *Wonderful Merciful Saviour,* Lyrics by Dawn Rodgers & Eric Wyse © Warner/Chappell Music, Inc

3. *I'm No Longer a Slave to Fear,* Bethel Music (2015)

CHAPTER THREE

THE LAW OF FIRST MENTION

There is a principle used in understanding Bible truths called, *The Law of First Mention*. Theologians and Bible teachers use this law to establish precedence and gain insight into original intent. The question is: When was the word *Worship* first mentioned in the bible?

Throughout biblical history, people have accorded some worth and reverence to God without using the word *Worship*. For instance, in Genesis 4, we read about the sacrifice of two brothers, Cain and Abel. At the end of the chapter, we read that *"men began to call upon the name of THE LORD"* (Genesis 4:26). We also read that *"Enoch walked with God..."* (Genesis 5:22); Noah also *"walked with God."* (Genesis 6:9). All these acts present to us ideas of "worship."

However, the first time the word *worship* was mentioned in the Bible was when Abraham offered Isaac to God on mount Moriah.

> [1]And it came to pass after these things, that God did tempt Abraham, and said unto him, Abraham: and he said, Behold, here I am.
>
> [2]And he said, take now thy son, thine only son Isaac, whom thou lovest, and get thee into the land of Moriah; and ***offer him there for a burnt offering*** upon one of the mountains which I will tell thee of.
>
> [3]And Abraham rose up early in the morning, and saddled his ass, and took two of his young men with him, and Isaac his son, and clave the wood for the burnt offering, and rose up, and went unto the place of which God had told him.
>
> [4]Then on the third day Abraham lifted up his eyes and saw the place afar off.
>
> [5]And Abraham said unto his young men, abide ye here with the ass; and I and the

> lad will go yonder and **WORSHIP** and come again to you.
>
> **Genesis 22:1-5**

Let us first note, in this scripture, the link between *offering* or *sacrifice* and *worship.* God told Abraham to go up a mountain and offer his only son, Isaac, as a sacrifice, and Abraham termed this *Worship*. What does this teach us? Ultimately, worship cannot take place without a life that is fully sacrificed unto Him.

> ***#Lesson:*** *My devotion to Him is my worship!*

In the scripture above, it is evident that what God wanted was not Abraham's son; He was testing him for his love and allegiance to Himself (God). If my heart is sold out to God, I will do anything for Him. Abraham loved and trusted God to the extent that he dared not question what seemed like a contradiction of promises God had previously given him on two separate ocassions.

> And the LORD took him outside and said, "Now look to the heavens and count the stars, if you are able." Then He declared,

> "So shall your offspring be."
>
> **Genesis 15:5**

> As for me, behold, my covenant is with thee, and thou shalt be a father of many nations.
>
> **Genesis 17:4**

Although it seemed like sacrificing his only son would result in the annulment of the promises God made to him, the promise of becoming a father of many nations, Abraham's undiluted commitment to God made him oblige to God's demand. Note again how he referred to the offering of his son as *worship.* The idea here is that anything I "lose" to God or for God is an act of worship!

> ***#Lesson:*** *worship is never about us but all about Him, our Maker, our Redeemer and our Lover!*

ISRAEL: SAVED FOR A PURPOSE OTHER THAN SELF!

The *first* time we see God deal with a group of people as His own was in the case of Israel, of whom we are spiritually a part. In Exodus 3:7-

12, we are given a clear picture of God's intention for saving His people.

> [7]And the LORD said, I have surely seen the affliction of my people which are in Egypt, and have heard their cry by reason of their taskmasters; for I know their sorrows;
>
> [8]And I am come down to deliver them out of the hand of the Egyptians, and to bring them up out of that land unto a good land and a large, unto a land flowing with milk and honey; unto the place of the Canaanites, and the Hittites, and the Amorites, and the Perizzites, and the Hivites, and the Jebusites.
>
> [9]Now therefore, behold, the cry of the children of Israel is come unto me: and I have also seen the oppression wherewith the Egyptians oppress them.
>
> [10]Come now therefore, and I will send thee unto Pharaoh, that thou mayest bring forth my people the children of Israel out of Egypt.
>
> [11]And Moses said unto God, who am I, that I should go unto Pharaoh, and that I should bring forth the children of Israel out of Egypt?

> [12]And he said, Certainly I will be with thee; and this shall be a token unto thee, that I have sent thee: When thou hast brought forth the people out of Egypt, ye shall serve God upon this mountain.
>
> **Exodus 3:7-12**

Clearly, the Lord had His agenda and reason for saving you and I: *"to serve (worship) him on this mountain."* In other words, we are saved so we can live a life that is wholly and completely dedicated to Him. As the sheep of His pasture, our choices and commitments should all be subjective to His will.

The afflictions of the Israelites in the hands of the Egyptians is symbolic of where you and I used to be - under the shackles of sin and Satan. We were under filth and condemnation, but God heard our cry, saved us and brought us into a *"good and a large land - a land flowing with milk and honey."* His goal for our salvation is to make us a people unto Himself; a people who will pledge and pay allegiance unto Him, fellowshipping with Him daily. This is what worship is all about!

> [2]I am the Lord thy God, which have brought thee out of the land of Egypt, out of the house of bondage.

> [3]Thou shalt have no other gods before me.
>
> [4]Thou shalt not make unto thee any graven image, or any likeness of anything that is in heaven above, or that is in the earth beneath, or that is in the water under the earth.
>
> **Exodus 20:2-4**

OUR LORD IS A JEALOUS GOD

Word Study: Jealous

Below is a brief study of the word, *Jealous.*

1. *Feeling or showing a resentful suspicion that one's partner is attracted to or involved with someone else. E.g. a jealous husband.*
2. *Fiercely protective of one's rights or possessions.*

Synonyms include: protective, defensive, vigilant, watchful, heedful, mindful, careful, solicitous, attentive.

I like the second definition because it portrays God in the right light - defensive, protective caring and committed to us! This is why He cannot share you with anything and anyone else! The Father requires our FULL allegiance to Him. He detests it when we fail to pursue His agenda and rather focus on ourselves. He needs our top attention and nothing else.

> **#Lesson:** *We are worship. Our worship lives cannot be dissociated or detached from our devotional lives and our relationship with God.*

Worship is therefore not simply what we do on stage or within the congregation on Sundays or at any Christian gathering. All these are just a confirmation of what we would have done with God and for Him in our closets or private lives. The time we spend with God, mostly alone and out of public view, means a lot to God than what we do in the congregation or on stage as singers or musicians. That said, one should be reflective of the other.

We deceive ourselves if we live like pagans outside the church environment and act pious whenever we are in are in church settings. May we receive the grace to daily offer our full attention to God, if we truly profess to be His. How do we do this? One of the effective ways is to devote much, if not all, attention to God. We will now explore this in the next chapter. Please come with me!

CHAPTER FOUR

THE DEVOTIONAL LIFE

The Ultimate Touchstone for Your Worship Life

The typical 21st century Christian is saddled with many distractions that take our attention away from God. It has become too easy to make gods out of worldly concerns and pleasure, including our careers, friends, families and other pastimes. We are prone to putting other things before God and have so little time for Him. We all must be forewarned!

During my secondary school days in Ghana, West Africa, I joined a Christian group called *Scripture Union (SU)*. This group was very radical. They taught young people to commit to God in a special way. One of the habits that I picked up from the SU was the culture of *Quiet Time*. I was a boarding student and we had the habit of checking on each other to make sure we were up to date with our quiet times. I love the healthy competitions that existed too. Whenever we met, someone would almost always be put on the spot to share something from their Quiet Time for that day. Knowing that everyone used the same devotional kept us on our toes. You could not just make up a story about what you learnt for the day. If you had not observed your Quiet Time, it would not be long before you are found out!

I thank God for those experiences. They left an indelible mark on my Christian life, even the habit of fellowshipping with God first thing in the morning. I only pray for the youth of today, especially those growing up in First World countries. They have become so dependent on technology and entertainment at the expense of a personal relationship with God. May God intervene and meet them in His own special ways.

#Lesson: *My devotional life measures my level of worship.*

THE QUIET TIME

Quiet Time is a regular, daily, private session of spiritual activities, such as prayer, meditation, worship and Bible study. The term "Quiet Time" was used by 20th-century Protestants, mostly evangelical Christians. It is also called "personal Bible study" or "personal devotions."

Christ is our perfect example of one who nurtured a devotional life. He had a culture of spending *quality* time with God in the best time of day (mornings), free from distractions. In fact, he would often retreat to a secluded place where the crowed that sought him for miracles, his own family or even his disciples could not find Him. We must all strive to perfect our devotional lives by looking unto Jesus (Hebrews 12:2a).

> **Very early** in the morning, while it was still dark, Jesus got up, **left the house** and went off to a **solitary** place, where **he prayed**.
>
> **Mark 1:35 NIV**

The *solitary* place, in our circumstances, could mean switching off our TV sets, phones, or other devices so we can be in tune with our God. We will consider these later. The question is: *what lessons can we derive from this verse?*

THE TIME

Jesus rose up early, still much in the night! The early hours of the day are the *firstfruits* of each day. They are the most precious moments of the day; times when noise is at the barest minimum, the brain can function at its best and the heart is alert to hear from God. Personally, I am attuned to God mostly when I am alone in the early hours, from midnight onwards, when the kids are asleep! A lot of times when I have heard an instruction from God, it was during one of these precious times!

THE ACTION

Jesus *"left the house and went off."* The *house* here is symbolic of all entanglements. First on the list would be our families or people we live with, followed by anything else, like *house* chores or commitments that grab our attention at home. Jesus retreated from all of these and went off!

Sometimes we need to *intentionally withdraw* ourselves from all work commitments and home duties just to enter that solitary and secret place where we can meet our God! Do not get me wrong; I am not advocating apathy or laziness at work. We need to justify our earnings by working diligently! However (borrowing the words of my husband who pastors our local church), when we take a break from work, which we all do anyway, we must intentionally plan to have a more intimate time with God!

Often, we pack our holidays or annual leaves with fun activities that keep us busy—even though we are meant to be resting and reflecting! Amidst such noise and *busy-ness,* we may not be in tune enough to hear from God even if He speaks to us. Jesus *left* His entanglements and *went off* to a secret place. When was the last time you went on a personal retreat to seek God on your own, not because you are in need of a miracle, but because you love Him and want to experience more of Him? Now, that is *worship,* a declaration that God is worthy of your time and attention. I challenge you to cultivate this practice and you will see what God can do with a heart that pants after Him!

THE PLACE

Jesus *"went off to a solitary place."* He separated Himself from the crowd, the noise and the attention. This is what I call being "alone with God." Sometimes, our worship and prayers do not get anywhere because we are not *alone* with God; we are still surrounded by the crowd, gadgets and other distractions. We do not have an *isolated place* where we meet God.

It is good practice to have a specially designated place, a closet if possible, for meeting with God. If space is an issue, a place in your bedroom would do. The atmosphere in which we connect with God is crucial. It determines whether or not we truly get to meet Him. What atmosphere have you created to meet God? You would need to put some concerted effort into this in the knowledge that God *"is a rewarder of those who **diligently** seek Him"* (Hebrews 11:6). Worship is about seeking God. Worship is about intimacy with God. Worship is about *building* a relationship with God. If we diligently seek Him, He will reward us.

May we prioritise our time effectively and efficiently to maximise our outputs in our worship lives. And to all those diligently seeking Him, may we be REWARDED in Jesus Name Amen!

QUIET TIME RESOURCES

There are several valuable materials, both online and in print that you can use to help enhance your Quiet Time. A lot of word-based churches have developed their bespoke resources, comprising of scriptural verses, commentaries, exhortations, declarations and prayers. Non-denominational bodies also produce devotional resources. The SU, whom I mentioned earlier, produce the annual *Daily Power* and *Daily Guide*, for youth and adults respectively; the *United Christian Broadcasters (UCB)*, a UK based charity, also produce the *Word for You* and *Word for Today* on a quarterly basis for youth and adults respectively. There are online versions that you can access.

Nevertheless, the list of resources would be incomplete without the following: A good study Bible, a notebook, pen/pencil and a highlighter. The best way to have an insight into God's word is through your own direct reading of the scriptures! And to help you remember what God tells you through His Word, you will need to take notes.

COMMON OBSTRUCTIONS TO OUR DEVOTIONAL LIVES

Work patterns, social status (which include family commitments) and social media are a few among an unending list of obstructions to our worship lives. Let us consider each of these three shortfalls and how they hinder our walk with God.

WORK PATTERNS

Compared with the time and energy spent on other things, the average 21st century Christian seems apathetic, droopy and uninterested in developing his or her spiritual walk with God. Sadly, we tend to use our jobs, businesses or careers as an excuse for not spending time with God! However, there is nowhere in scripture where God indulged people who put Him on the second rung of their priority list.

Generally, everyone God called and saved, from the Old to the New Testament, had a job, business, career or interest that they were pursuing before he saved. Abraham was an idol worshipper when God called him; Moses was tending his father-in-law's sheep when he encountered God. The apostles in the New testament were all professionals in their own rights when Jesus called them to follow Him. Yet, when they heeded the call of God, their jobs or social status did not stand in the way of their walk with God. Their walk with God was prioritised over other commitments.

Admittedly, we all need God's grace on a daily basis to prioritise our walk with Him, maintain a consistent devotional life and have a healthy work-life balance without relegating God to the background. This is possible. There are thousands of Christians who have developed consistent devotional lifestyles, and so can you! More grace to us! Yet, I believe that we disappoint Him when we let our jobs, careers and personal businesses take His place in our lives. This is particularly so if the first thing you do when you wake up in the morning is to jump out of bed and go straight into *your* business. No devotional time. No mediation. No prayer. No Bible reading. In short, NO TIME FOR GOD!

I have observed, from personal ministry experiences, that this apathetic lifestyle is prevalent among Christians in the diaspora, particularly the western world. (Needless to say, there is the other extreme where believers engage in empty religiosities at the expense of work and productivity. This is a topic for another day!).

#Lesson: *Every true worshipper loves to spend time with God.*

We make time for things we love. In the same way, if we truly love God, we will delight in His presence and carve out time to be with Him. Often, people who give excuses for not participating in the gatherings of the saints do not actually love God. They hardly pray, worship or study the scriptures on their own either! Their excuse for lacking intimacy with God is the same reason why they cannot attend church or a spiritual gathering.

Ironically, these same people find the time to spend at parties, funerals and other social gatherings. They never use their jobs, careers or businesses as excuses not to attend. How hypocritical we can sometimes be as humans!

We need to be *real* with God. When we identify and acknowledge our weaknesses, rather than pretend all is well, God will give us grace to overcome them. However, show me a God-addict and I will show you one who, in spite of work commitments, finds time to relate with and worship his or her Maker!

SOCIAL STATUS AND CONNECTIONS

Social status and connections, whether *achieved* or *ascribed,* can be a major stumbling block to our worship lives. People get into social positions or rankings either as a result of their achievements (what they work for or attain through study) or through ascribed means (fixed or inherited through birth, sex, age, race, ethnicity or family background). However, irrespective of how status is attained, some become attached to certain cultures, privileges and lifestyles associated with their status, thus inhibiting their connection to the MAKER who brought them to this world.

I have seen people who were as down as the earth when they were "nobodies." They were very spiritual, holy and committed to the things of God, until the same God began to bless and enlarge them! These same people began to shift their loyalty from God to their spouses, children, clicks of friends, job colleagues, businesses and everything else but God. They would rather go with the multitude—their friends and connections—rather than spend time in God's presence and hear from Him. In fact, social clicks and connections have robbed many Christians of the privilege to hear from God. No wonder there is a lot of carnal, fleshy and erotic Christians nowadays who are so insensitive to the dealings of the Holy Spirit.

When we come to God, irrespective of our social status, we need to *leave* our old ways and connections and *cleave* unto His ways. If we do not do this, we can neither relate to nor worship Him the way He wants us to.

One man who demonstrated this *leaving* and *cleaving* requirement in our relationship with God is Abraham.

> [1]Now the Lord had said to Abram: "Get out of your country, from your family and from your father's house, to a land that I will show you.
>
> [2]I will make you a great nation; I will bless you and make your name great; and you shall be a blessing.
>
> [3]I will bless those who bless you, and I will curse him who curses you; and in you all the families of the earth shall be blessed."
>
> [4]So Abram departed as the Lord had spoken to him, and Lot went with him. And Abram was seventy-five years old when he departed from Haran.
>
> **Genesis 12:1-4 NKJV**

God called Abraham from idolatry unto salvation, that he may become a blessing to the world. God told Him to *"get out of his country, his family and his father's house."* These were his connections, people and cultures he had grown with for 75 years. As we know, Abraham came from an inherited (ascribed) background of idolatry. However, he heard God tell him to move out and he did not not hesitate to sever himself from his clicks.

I believe it was not easy for Abraham to disconnect himself from the way of life he had been used to all his life. Nobody said it was going to be easy to let go of a long-standing friendship, association or relationship that has been a part of your life for years. But if those connections are getting in the way of your walk with God and your destiny, it is better to let them go. The naming and shaming you might suffer for leaving them can never be compared to the glory that lies ahead of your obedience to your divine mandate.

Do not be afraid to lose friends and clicks if that is what you have to do to fulfil your divine assignment. Ultimately, you shall be made great among the same people who despised you for switching your allegiance to God! Abraham did the unpopular thing and left his kindred. Even in the face of ridicule, he *cleaved* to God and the blessings of God followed his obedience to the divine call.

> [7]Then the Lord appeared to Abram and said, "To your descendants I will give this land." And there he built an altar to the Lord, who had appeared to him
>
> [8]...and called on the name of the Lord.
>
> **Genesis 12:7-8**

When Abraham heeded God's call, he "built an altar to the lord and called on the name of the Lord." In other words, he worshipped, adored and expressed his love to God. You see, salvation and connection to God is always followed by worship! Abraham caught the revelation that he was called out by God to *worship* Him. We were saved to worship God alone.

> [17]Therefore, "Come out from among them and be separate, says the Lord. Do not touch what is unclean, and I will receive you."
>
> [18]"I will be a Father to you, and you shall be My sons and daughters, says the LORD Almighty."
>
> **2 Corinthians 6:17-18**

SOCIAL MEDIA EXCESSES

We live in a technologically-advanced world, which has made access to a lot of things pretty a lot easier compared to previous generations. This is good, generally. I believe that Social media is part of the advancements that God has allowed for humanity. It has contributed to development in diverse ways, including the spiritual growth of many Christians, mine as well. Preachers and worshippers have used social media to spread the gospel and win many to Christ. Moreover, there is the recreational and humorous side of it that we all need at times. I am not opposed to these at all.

However, there are real tendencies to abuse or overuse this medium, a practice that is ripping the average Christian off their connection with God. I think something needs to be done urgently!

Consider the following:

Social media has grown tremendously in the last few years. From 2006 onwards the growth rate is unexpectedly very high. Specially Facebook and Twitter have grown much faster and captured millions of users in just a few years. The way technology is growing, it is obvious that more and more people are going to grasp its benefits. It has brought a lot of advantages for the society. From progressed nations to under-developed countries, every nation is utilizing the power of social media to enhance life and use it for the bitterness of the people.

However, on the other hand it has also affected the society in the negative way. ***Just like anything which can be used for both good and bad, social media have also provided the negative and positive ways for the people. It is all about the usage and getting things done positively by using the power of social media. It is in the hands of the user to use to its advantage.*** *But willingly or unwillingly it can still be used to create negative impacts on the users or recipients.*[1]

What are the disadvantages of social media? I am focusing on the disadvantages because, as we know, everything was originally created with the good of users in mind. However, when a concept or an idea is used wrongly, we experience its disadvantages.

For the purpose of this text, I will briefly mention five pitfalls of social media and explore the last in more detail. Social media does not only affect our devotional lives, it presents an array of quagmires, including the following:

1. Health Issues

The excessive use of social media can have a negative impact on a person's health. Neglecting the need to exercise and maintain their fitness, many social media users become lazy as they spend time on social networking sites.

2. Glamourising Evil

One of the disadvantages of social media is that people follow others who are wealthy or addicted to drugs by sharing their views and videos on the web. This inspires others to follow suit and end up experimenting with or getting addicted to the same substances.

3. Ruining Reputations

Social media can easily be the means to ruin a person's reputation through the creation and broadcasting a false stories. Similarly, businesses can also suffer losses due to bad reputation being conveyed over the social media.

4. Cheating in Relationships

Many have used social media platforms to meet and marry their spouse. However, after a while, some realise they have made wrong decisions either because their so-called "lovers" were not who they thought them to be. They, therefore, end up parting ways.

Similarly, some couples have cheated on each other by flirting with others behind their partners' back and pretending nothing has happened. Some of the things you will hear happening in relation-ships because of social media are simply abominable. Lord have mercy!

5. *Addiction*

The addictive tendencies of social media cannot be overemphasised. It is one of the subtlest "stealers" of time. Many Christians are constantly hooked on social media for most of their day, at the expense of their intimate time with God. Needless to say, young people, teenagers in particular, are mostly affected by the canker of social media addiction. They get involved very extensively and are eventually cut off from the society in terms of real socialising. For some teenagers, their phones are the first and last things they crave for each day.

However, the sad reality is that adults who are supposed to restrain, guide and direct these youngsters toward the right actions are equally guilty—and in some cases, guiltier! How can we spur one another unto love and good works (Hebrews 10:24)?

THE SAD REALITY

Some grown-up and matured Christian, on a daily basis, connect with their phones, tablets and other devices for socialisation, much more than they talk to God, their wives, husbands or children - the most important entities in their lives. What is your first point of call when you wake up? What do you connect with first thing in the morning? Your phone or prayer?

I strive as much as possible not to check my phone for messages until I have rendered my "Good Morning Lord" service! This is what pledging allegiance to the Lord is all about—prioritising God above every other thing including friends and acquaintances on Facebook, Instagram or Twitter!

You can relegate that social media platform to the background and spend precious, quality time with your Father without any distractions. Just like Jesus, *intentionally* retreat from that phone or tablet until you have had that 'alone' time with Him.

Clearly, the unfortunate imbalance and misappropriation of time is wrong in the eyes of the One who called us. You should not be so much glued to your social media platforms to the extent that they become your first point of call in the morning, even before you say a prayer or read the Bible!

#Lesson: *If we want to be attuned with the Holy Spirit; if we want to be on God's radar and frequency; if we want to hear from God constantly, then we must sometimes "switch off" from the noise on Facebook, Instagram, WhatsApp and friends on call! God does not want to compete with anyone or anything in our lives.*

Prayer

Father, please give us the grace to please you with our devotional lives even in the face of these perilous chaotic, distractive times that we find ourselves Amen!

1. https://www.techmaish.com/advantages-and-disadvantages-of-social-media-for-society/

CHAPTER FIVE

LESSONS FROM THE TABERNACLE

On Mount Sinai, God invited Moses to spend some time with Him. During their time together, God gave Moses two sets of systems, namely the *system of law* (The Ten Commandments) and the *system of sacrifice* (major insignias for worship). He instructed that these two systems be placed within a building called the Tabernacle. The idea was that God had set rules for His people, but because He knew they would break them, He provided a way so they would not die but remain "alive" in Him.

I have done a detailed exposition of the tabernacle, which would be part of another book;

but for the purpose of this work, the following is a brief summary, as it relates to the *Worth-ship mandate.*

The Tabernacle of Moses[1]

DEFINITION & PURPOSE

Word Study: Tabernacle

The Merriam Webster's Dictionary offers three distinct but similar definitions for the noun *Tabernacle* (/ˈtabəˌnak(ə)l/). For the purpose of our study, I have stated all three below.

1. A house of worship; specifically, a large building or tent used for evangelistic services.

2. A receptacle for the consecrated elements of the Eucharist; especially: an ornamental locked box used for reserving the Communion hosts.

3. Often capitalised: (a) tent sanctuary used by the Israelites during the Exodus; (b) archaic: a dwelling place; (c) archaic: a temporary shelter: tent.

The Tabernacle was first mentioned in the book of Exodus, while Israel wandered in the wilderness. As mentioned above, God instructed Moses to build Him a place where He could dwell in the midst of His people. This was a temporary building because it was meant to foreshadow His plan to dwell in the hearts of man. In other words, the Tabernacle was to demonstrate God's desire to have a sustainable relationship with His people at all times.

SPECIFICATIONS

The Tabernacle was built *strictly* according to God's own specifications.

> [8]Let them construct a sanctuary for Me, that I may dwell among them.
>
> [9]According to all that I am going to show you, as the pattern of the tabernacle and the pattern of all its furniture, just so you shall construct it.
>
> **Exodus 25:8-9 NASB**

This goes to show that God is particular about the purpose and practice of worship. He did not leave the construction of the Tabernacle to Moses' discretion. He gave Moses detailed guidelines on what to do and how to build.

The actual specifications and details of the Tabernacle, as given by God to Moses 3,500 years ago are contained in Exodus 26. The layout of the Tabernacle was later replicated in Jerusalem when Solomon built the first temple. It too had a courtyard or porches, then a Holy Place, and a Holy of Holies, where only the high priest could enter once a year, on the Day of Atonement. Early Christian churches followed the same general pattern, with an outer court or inside lobby, a sanctuary, and an inner tabernacle where the communion elements were kept. Roman Catholic, Eastern Orthodox and Anglican churches and cathedrals retain similar features today!

Both the exterior and interior architecture and furnishings of the Tabernacle were intentional and purposeful. They all conveyed distinct messages from the heart of God. In fact, the design and emblems of the Tabernacle foreshadowed and projected into the future—including the emergence of the New Testament church. It would amaze you to see how Christ, concealed in the Old Testament but revealed in the New, forms such an important *cornerstone* of our worship lives.

Suffice to say that the Old Testament points to the person of Jesus (when He became flesh) dwelling among us. All the parts of the Tabernacle, as well as its furniture, looked forward to and represented our Saviour, Jesus Christ, and His redemptive work.

The Tabernacle *was "not only to be a sign of God's presence with, and protection of his people, but his habitation or dwelling-place among them: the place where he would, in a peculiar manner, manifest his presence, display his glory, accept their oblations, prayers, praises, and other services, and by the intervention of Moses and Aaron first, and afterward of the high-priest for the time being, would communicate to them his mind and will."*[2]

PLACES & EMBLEMS

From the specifications given in the scripture above, we can infer that the Tabernacle, made mainly with expensive and durable acacia (shittim) wood, had four designated places: *Outside, Outer Courtyard, Holy Place* and *Holy of Holies,* as well as ten emblems or insignias: *Entrance gate, Altar of Burnt offerings, Laver, Door to the Holy Place, Table of Shewbread, The Bread, Menorah, The Veil, Altar of Incense* and *Ark of Covenant with Shekinah*). These four places and each of the ten emblems are significant in pointing us to Christ and enriching our worship. The following is a brief summary of these aspects of the Tabernacle *(Please look out for an in-depth analysis of the details in my next book).*

THE FOUR AREAS OF THE TABERNACLE

1. *Outside*

This was made of white linen walls, high enough to make it impossible to 'jump' over it and low enough to prevent someone creeping into the sanctuary. The sanctuary is protected against "thieves," and everyone *outside* is outside God's presence!

2. *Outer Courtyard*

This is the first place a person will stand after entering the Tabernacle. This is where our initial acts of praise begins.

3. *Holy Place*

Originally only accessible by priests, but now open to all New Testament believers because of the work of Jesus on the cross. Here, we perform our priestly duties of ministering unto the Lord.

> But ye are a chosen generation, a royal priesthood, an holy nation, a peculiar people; that ye should shew forth the praises of him who hath called you out of darkness into his marvellous light.
>
> **2 Peter 2:9**

4. Holy of Holies

This is the final and most intimate place, made up of a single room and only accessible by one special person—the high priest—who would plead forgiveness on behalf of all Israel year on year. We now have a better covenant, in that Christ is our High Priest who pleads daily for us! In our worship, this is the place where we hear God speak to us! I must say that we do not always get to this stage in both our individual and corporate worship; it takes potency, passion, patience, perseverance and purposefulness to get here, and you must be one!

TEN SYMBOLS IN THE TABERNACLE

1. Entrance Gate

Everyone *must* come through here. With its four colours of purple, blue, scarlet (red) and white, we see Jesus featured in His royalty (purple), divinity (blue), atonement (scarlet) and purity (white). Without Him, our worship is worthless.

2. *Altar of burnt offering*

The first activity of sacrifice takes place here. Our old selves must be put to death if we are to please Him with our worship. We are to be *"living sacrifices, holy and pleasing unto Him"* (Romans 12:1b).

3. *Laver*

This is the place of sanctification, where we are cleansed by God's word. Our minds are transformed, the flesh overcome and we receive grace to enter in. True worship begins here!

4. *Door*

The next stage of entrance, which is also a reminder of the Gate.

5. *Table of Shewbread*

At this place, the word of God comes alive. This is where revelation is received.

6. The bread on the table

This is Rhema, God's fresh Word. We minister unto the Lord in declarations and proclamations at this stage.

7. Menorah

This is the Golden lampstand, the only source of light in the Holy place, representing Jesus Christ, the light of God's presence. From this place, we draw strength and gain insight. The Holy Spirit, who is the representative of Christ on the earth and who dwells in us, gives us illumination here.

8. The Veil

This is a reference to the law that hid a holy God from sinful people. Its colours again refer to Christ.

9. Altar of Incense

This refers to sacrifice and total surrender.

10. Ark of Covenant with Shekinah

This gold-plaited wooden box contains the gold jar of manna, Aaron's staff that had budded, and the stone tablets of the covenant. The cherubim of the Glory sat above the ark.

When deep worship goes up, His glory is revealed and every need is met!

Note: *I have done a thorough study of each aspect of this enigmatic edifice in my next book! Look out for it!*

---

1. www.freebibleimages.org/illustrations/moses-tabernacle/

2. Benson's Commentary

CHAPTER SIX

THANKSGIVING, PRAISE & WORSHIP

One of the mysteries I have sought the Holy Spirit to unravel to me is whether there is a definite answer to this intriguing question: What are the differences, if any, between *thanksgiving, praise* and *worship*? After years of searching, I have come to the conclusion that the three are distinct, but they also work together in a synchronised manner, just like the marriage pact.

This is similar to all other faith practices, such us tithing, prayer, studying the Word etc. You cannot separate one from the other! That is what makes Christianity stand out from the rest. It is, indeed, a lifestyle and not merely a belief. In this chapter, I am going to try and draw out the distinct features of each stage of our devotion.

THANKSGIVING

Simply put, thanksgiving is an expression of gratitude to God. This means, thanksgiving is a response to something God has *done* for or to us. Surely, you can point to something God has done for you! Can you remember how God came through for you when you needed His help?

Yes, *when we remember what someone has done for us, we show them appreciation.* Remembering the favour also leads to you *praise* the person. Therefore, in practice, our praise is oftentimes intertwined with thanksgiving. Both can happen simultaneously. Remembering the Lord's goodness stirs us to come into the place of His dwelling.

It takes remembrance to appreciate a person. This is why ungrateful people are often those who forget! The moment you forget how good a person has been to you, showing gratitude to them will not come readily. This applies to all facets of life.

Realise then, my friend, that we all need to work on ourselves to keep a fresh memory of the kindness people have shown to us in order to keep a healthy relationship with them. In the same vein, we must keep our minds on the goodness of the Lord. In fact, remembering those who have done good to you is part of the lessons God teaches us in life so that we could return the same gratitude (and even more) to Him. Forgetful people are dangerous people; they can be as treacherous as the devil himself! Don't forget what the Lord has done.

The song writer, Johnson Oatman Jr. (1856-1926), said:

When upon life's billows you are tempest tossed,
When you are discouraged, thinking all is lost,
Count your many blessings name them one by one,
And it will surprise you what the Lord hath done.

Chorus

Count your blessings, name them one by one;
Count your blessings, see what God hath done;
Count your blessings, name them one by one,
And it will surprise you what the Lord hath done.

Are you ever burdened with a load of care?
Does the cross seem heavy you are called to bear?
Count your many blessings, every doubt will fly,
And you will be singing as the days go by.[1]

Word study: Thank

A quick study of the verb *thank* reveals a relationship between the word and two other words: *mercy* and *grace.* How beautiful! The French translates "thank" as *merci* and grace for the English word "mercy." The Spanish translation of "thank" is *gracias,* which is synonymous with the word grace in English.

The benefits of being thankful

If you are a parent, a leader or someone with jurisdiction over people, you will bear witness to this: whenever your child or subordinate shows appreciation for a kindness you have shown to them, it sparks off some more generosity and affection towards them, doesn't it? And you are either intentionally or sometimes unintentionally drawn to that person to the extent that it could be judged as favouritism by others on the same par with them! This is the reality of life. Everything we go through in life is supposed to teach us how the Lord wants to relate with us. When you are thankful, you gain more favour from God!

We are the beneficiaries if we choose to maintain a thankful attitude towards God! Yes, being thankful is our first step into His presence.

> **Enter into his gates with thanksgiving**, and into his courts with praise: be thankful unto him and bless his name.
>
> **Psalm 100:4**

PRAISE

As much as it takes remembrance to be thankful, it takes remembrance to be 'praiseful' too! As I said, earlier, the two: "thanksgiving and praises" work together closely. They are intertwined. When you are thankful, your heart will also begin to swell happily towards God. This is why I believe that during congregational worship, we must go through these two processes before entering into worship! We enter the gates (of the Tabernacle) with thanksgiving, then proceed to the courts with praises to the rock of our salvation.

As quoted above, Psalm 100:4 sets the procedure clearly: *Enter into his gates with thanksgiving,* ***and into his courts with praise:*** *be thankful unto him and bless his name.*

One of my fathers of faith, Derek Prince recounts three timeless reasons for thanking and praising God:

- Thank and praise God for His mercies (He is merciful).

- Thank and praise God for His creation (He made you and all that nature provides).
- Thank and praise God for His goodness.

During praises, which happens in the courts, our eyes are open; we can see everyone around; we can see God's creation too - the trees, the skies, the beauties of nature, and we can use our imaginations to appreciate His creation and praise Him for it. Praise is often boisterous, lively and energetic. This is because, we show how excited we are about God and His doings. It is, as Don Moen, one of my favourite worship leaders, describes: a monologue (one-way speech) where we, God's children, talk to Him and makes Him feel good about Himself. Here, we recount all His goodness and affirm His majesty and Lordship. This is where we begin to create an atmosphere for Him to respond to us. As we delve deeper in praise, especially during high praises, we are able to enter the warfare zone where our praise turns into a weapon on our behalf!

Sometimes, while leading worship, I sense an aura of freedom and liberation as if our Father is ready to go on a war on our behalf. On such occasions, I would stop the music and get us to enter into intercession straight away!

This is what Jesus meant when he taught His disciples how to pray in Matthew 6:9-13: Power praise and worship must precede intercession if we want to see results.

Praise is a powerful weapon. Praise pleases God. It moves Him. So before you lift up intercession, lift up thanksgiving and praise. As one of my favourite singers, Tasha Cobbs, sang: Put a praise on it:

There's a miracle in this room

With my name on it

There's a healing in this room

And it's is here for me

There's a breakthrough in this room

With my name on it

So what you gone do

I'm gonna put a praise on it

So I'm gonna put a praise on it

Beloved, some problems and challenges we face in life rear their ugly heads for destruction! What am I saying? Some of the challenges we face are actually God's way of giving us the opportunity to *destroy* them through the powerful weapon of praise and worship. So, when you consider your problems, say to them "you have indeed come for your destruction!" Expectant praise (praising God ahead of a miracle you are expecting) moves Him to go ahead and fight for you. It might not make sense, but it works and that settles it. No arguments here! Jehoshaphat led Isreal in a prophetic power praise when they were surrounded by their enemies, Moab and Ammon. And guess what happened?

> [21]And when he had consulted with the people, he appointed singers unto the LORD, and that should praise the beauty of holiness, as they went out before the army, and to say, Praise the LORD; for his mercy endureth for ever.
>
> [22]And when they began to sing and to praise, the LORD set ambushments against the children of Ammon, Moab, and mount Seir, which were come against Judah; and they were smitten.
>
> [23]For the children of Ammon and Moab stood up against the inhabitants of mount Seir, utterly to slay and destroy them: and when they had made an end of the inhabitants of Seir, every one helped to destroy another.
>
> [24]And when Judah came toward the watch

> tower in the wilderness, they looked unto the multitude, and, behold, they were dead bodies fallen to the earth, and none escaped.

May none of your enemies escape as you begin to lead a praiseful lifestyle in Jesus' name, Amen.

Stop worrying. Start praising now! Say, "Here is my praise. Please Lord, give me my miracle!"

WORSHIP

Worship is about intimacy, comparable to the relationship between a man and his wife. I see praise and thanksgiving as the foreplay that happens between married people, prior to getting intimate. Worship is the climax. This is the ultimate destination. This is where it must all end.

Worship only happens when we enter the Holy place and push further into the Holy of Holies. As thanksgiving is intertwined with praise, worship is intertwined with surrender. While praise involves our outward selves and emotions, worship deals with our inner selves. Our attitude during worship shows our spiritual state and how connected we are to the Father. Practically, each step into the tent of meetings (the Tabernacle) drew people closer to the mercy seat where the glory of God hovered. This is where He spoke to the high priest who was the only one qualified to enter. But thank God for Jesus who has given everyone the opportunity to be a "High Priest"!

When we enter into worship, the Lord begins to minister to us. That is to say, He talks to us. He reveals our true selves. He shows us the things to alter, the changes to make in aspects of our lives, He gives directions and ideas etc. This explains why He instructed Moses to place the Ten Commandments in the Ark of the Covenant.

The Commandments represented God's instructions to Israel. Worship is based on the state of our hearts and how willing we are to listen to God. You cannot be a worshipper and not check your attitude and behaviour. If you are a worshipper, the Spirit checks you constantly and you submit unconditionally. You must be willing to say "sorry" when you miss the mark, not only with God, but more importantly with people. Checking our attitudes as worshippers is very vital to the success of what we do.

***#Truth:** A person can go through the outward motions of praise and join in singing songs with the congregation without necessarily worshipping.*

SOME THOUGHTFUL DISTINCTIONS

- Praise can be extended to other relationships.
- Worship must be reserved for God.
- Praise is easy, worship is not.
- Praise can play on our excitement; worship requires humility and holiness.
- Worship is about intimacy.
- Everyone at the courts can praise; not everyone gets into the holy place to worship.
- Through worship, we realign our priorities with God's.
- Worship is tangled with surrender.

1. *Count Your Blessings*, by Johnson Oatman Jr. (1856-1926)

CHAPTER SEVEN

THE CORRECT FORMAT FOR WORSHIP

[1]O come, let us sing unto the LORD: let us make **a joyful noise to the ROCK OF OUR SALVATION.**

[2]Let us come before his presence with **thanksgiving,** and make a joyful noise unto him with psalms.

[3]For the LORD is a great God, and a great King above all gods.

[4]In his hand are the deep places of the earth: the strength of the hills is his also.

[5]The **sea is his**, and he made it: and his hands formed the dry land.

[6]O come, let us worship and bow down: let us kneel before the LORD our maker.

[7]For he is our God; and we are the people of his pasture, and the sheep of his hand. To day if ye will hear his voice,

[8]Harden not your heart, as in the provocation, and as in the day of temptation in the wilderness:

[9]When your fathers tempted me, proved me, and saw my work.

[10]Forty years long was I grieved with this generation, and said, It is a people that do err in their heart, and they have not known my ways:

[11]Unto whom I sware in my wrath that they should not enter into my rest.

Psalm 95:1-11

This scripture, which offers us ideas about the pattern for worship, sums up the whole point of *why* we worship. There is a call for us to worship *one* Person (Jesus), for one major reason (for providing the foundation, the rock, of our salvation). The psalmist entreats us to "come and sing together and make joyful noise to THE ROCK OF OUR SALVATION."

The pronoun "us" suggest corporate worship. So, there is a place for corporate worship. As children of God, we are enjoined to connect our graces together and present our sacrifice of worship unto our Father.

Here, we are referring to a combination of actors, including singers, drummers, players of all kinds of musical accoutrements to create ONE SOUND in praising and worshiping our Father together. This is what we do whenever we gather in groups or in church. A typical example of corporate worship involving the creation of *one sound* can be found in the following scripture.

> [18]And Jehoshaphat bowed his head with his face to the ground: and all Judah and the inhabitants of Jerusalem fell before the Lord, worshipping the Lord.
>
> [19]And the Levites, of the children of the Kohathites, and of the children of the Korhites, stood up to praise the Lord God of Israel with **a loud voice on high**.
>
> [20]And they rose early in the morning, and went forth into the wilderness of Tekoa: and as they went forth, Jehoshaphat stood and said, Hear me, O Judah, and ye inhabitants of Jerusalem; Believe in the Lord

your God, so shall ye be established; believe his prophets, so shall ye prosper.

[21]And when he had consulted with the people, he appointed singers unto the Lord, and that should praise the beauty of holiness, as they went out before the army, and to say, Praise the Lord; for his mercy endureth for ever.

[22]And when they began to sing and to praise, the Lord set ambushments against the children of Ammon, Moab, and mount Seir, which were come against Judah; and they were smitten.

2 Chronicles 20:18-21

Here, we are entreated to uphold the spirit of unity in our purpose as worshipers. If our corporate worship will yield results such as the one witnessed in the days of Jehoshaphat, we must endeavour to present *one sound* to God!

What does it mean to present one sound? It means to have the same mindset without entertaining offences or disagreements; being in synchronisation with each player. This includes singers, technicians, ushers, pastors and everyone within the jurisdiction of the building where the worship service is happening. It is, therefore, not right for people to be doing "other things" when worship begins in church! Worship is one moment when God expects us all to engage in order to achieve results.

The above notwithstanding, we should not have to lose sight of the verb "come" used in Psalm 95. The idea here is that whether we are giving corporate worship of individual worship, we are all supposed to "come" through the same gate (Jesus Christ), through whom we are qualified to offer acceptable worship to God. *(Please look out for my detailed work on the GATE to the Tabernacle in my next book).*

CHAPTER EIGHT

STIMULI FOR WORSHIP

This chapter deals with the many incentives and catalysts that move the child of God into praise and worship.

In order for us to offer effective thanksgiving, praise and worship unto God, we must consciously utilise the advantages of both our spirit man (which is who we really are) and our body. These two parts of us must unite in order for us to be effective worshippers. By utilising our spirits, I am referring to consciously switching off from your environments and tuning in to connect with heaven - an effort and a choice we have to make.

Worship does not just take place with your mouth singing some songs or uttering some words; it is a work; a decision that requires corresponding effort. *You* decide to offer your worship. You have to *make* your spirit-man yearn to do so. If you are born of the water, the spirit and the blood, there is an inner witness within you, described by Paul in Romans 8:16a as follows: *The Spirit Himself bears witness with our spirit...(NKJV).* This inner witness causes you to rise and connect with God in worship.

It may start as an obligation, a chore or even a burden, especially when you are in an overwhelming situation; when you look around and cannot find anything tangible for which you must thank or worship God. Yet, as one born of His spirit, you will realise that you cannot help but burst out in a prayer or song of worship because, as we have studied earlier, our worship and praise is not necessarily based on what did or did not go well with us. Rather, it is that yearning or desire to relate with our Father, our husband, our Lord, first and foremost for Him giving us His son.

I always picture the *Son of God* so beautifully presented in the Tabernacle. Truly, our Praise and worship should be centred on Christ, the Son of God. This is why the world, unbelievers or even believers, who enjoy living in sin *cannot* offer acceptable worship! Please do not get me wrong; they can sing or even pray, but they cannot offer *acceptable* worship (remember the devil himself, the father of all evil, was the embodiment of music before his fall)! Yes, the word of God is clear on this; the type of worship God accepts is one offered *"in sprit and in truth."* As Jesus revealed, *"the Father seeks such to worship him"* (John 4:23b). Your spirit-man must be in agreement with God's standards prior to singing His song and worshiping.

EMOTIONS HELP BOOST WORSHIP

One beautiful Sunday, I listened to a lady give a testimony in church about a miracle she had received. This lady had trusted God to pass her driving licence test. She had invested a lot of money into preparing for it and failed in her previous test. Broken and gutted, the second attempt meant everything to her. So, she prayed and depended on God for success this time.

Thankfully, she passed and, in view of her prior bad experience, was full of joy. Then I made sense of why she was so excited and fully engaged during the worship session earlier in the service. You can probably testify of such moments when your prayer had been answered and you came to church to give some exceptional worship! Your joy got compounded because you received something you have trusted Him for—healing or a breakthrough of some kind. As Solomon wrote, *The desire accomplished is sweet to the soul* (Proverbs 13:19a).

Admittedly, our bodies sync with our spirits in offering worship. By utilising our bodies, I am referring to our senses and emotions, housed in our brains. So, in effect, when we get excited or pleased with something, it does and must reflect in our praise and worship.

I remember many times that my Sunday worship had been inspired by some kind of a miracle I had received the week before or so. I am sure you you can relate too! This said, we must graduate to the place where we offer absolute and exceptional worship *regardless* of situations. This, I must admit, takes a lot of spiritual weight. May the Lord help us all.

As God formed us in His own image, I believe God is emotional; He has feelings, just as we do. That means He can get excited, sad, angry etc. just as we do sometimes. What are the things that make you excited about your loved ones? What makes you tick? What puts you off somebody? What makes you stick to someone? Do you like to be appreciated when you have sacrificed something for someone? Do you feel loved and respected when someone you care for says kind words about you *to you?* If you said "yes" to these questions, then remember, the Lord feels the same and even more intensely, because He loves you with even more passion! Let us reflect on these questions and judge how God feels by our personal worship. This self-assessment will help us know where to improve in our worship lives. Apart from our primary reason for worship (being made heirs with Christ), we must endeavour to use our senses, especially our feelings, imaginations and thoughts, to help us appreciate His deeds in our lives.

CREATION GIVES US REASONS TO PRAISE

God made the heavens and the earth before forming man. This means, He did not only provide all that man would need before forming him, but also God ensured that man would have enough evidence to stimulate pure worship. All the beautiful aspects of nature are not only for our comfort, but also a memorial for our praise and worship. Psalm 95, which we looked at earlier, confirms this in the fourth and fifth verses; they talk about what we can see with our eyes as the doing of the Lord.

> [4]In his hand are the **deep places of the earth: the strength of the hills** is his also.
>
> [5]The **sea is his**, and he made it: and **his hands formed the dry land**.
>
> **Psalm 95:40-5**

God, our Maker, did created all these to help us *remember* and acknowledge His *worth.* Humans forget things easily. We lose sight of what is important. However, God's wonders in creation is a constant reminder of His greatness and glory!

Whenever you are overwhelmed or underwhelmed by situations, bored to the point where you are short of what to say in worship, think, ponder, look around you; there are so many evidences of His goodness that would simulate your worship!

CHAPTER NINE

REBECCA: MY WORSHIP LIFE

I was born into a church-going family. My siblings and I would always follow mum to church every now and then. We started from what we called Sunday School (Kids Church), progressed to the Youth Church and sometimes joining the adult services.

Some of the flagship church programmes—the ones I really enjoyed—were the Annual Easter Conventions, which attracted large audiences, thousands of people, in one venue. These were dramatic and spectacular moments of my childhood that still sit with me to date! For four days during each Easter, people from all the branches of my mother church, *The Apostolic Church, Ghana, West Africa,* travelled from all walks of life to a central place in Accra, the capital city, to celebrate the death and resurrection of Christ. It was such a time of refreshing, connecting and revival! I loved the long journeys to and from where we lived, especially travelling together on a bus. I had some liking for a God up there. I loved the music and I enjoyed the routine of attending church every Sunday. However, I was not sure, at that stage in my life, whether I had actually met or had an encounter with this God.

Suffice to say that despite my belief in God and participation in almost every church programme, I did not have a firm basis to support my beliefs. If I was challenged during those times or simply asked to justify my belief, I would be catapulted into the thin air in defeat. I truly did not know what I was doing! It was more a cultural thing than a life being lived.

THE TURNING POINT

All this changed during my secondary education, when I turned fifteen. I began to make a lot of sense out of the whole idea of having a relationship with God.

One day, in church, I said the sinner's prayers (still without really understanding deeply what it was all about). Afterwards, I kept going with the flow and joined the *Scripture Union (SU)* as a boarding student in the school I attended. I made friends and connected with likeminded students within the SU group and it was then I started to grow my faith. As I engaged in spiritual activities, I started drawing closer to God and having personal times with Him.

Soon, I found my place! I joined a music group called *The Golden Bells,* which gave me additional responsibilities not just as a nominal member, but also as a worker. Being a worker in God's vineyard helps your spiritual growth; if you do not have any responsibilities in your local church, your growth cannot be sustained.

I remember how we would "monitor" each other regarding our devotional lifestyles and how we indirectly "competed" among ourselves as to who read the bible the most! Oh how I miss those days and wish the present generation, especially those growing up in the developed world, will have such opportunities!

The SU had two devotionals, *Daily Bread* and *Daily Power*. Both were useful Bible study resources for the young and old. Decades down the line, I can remember vividly how impactful they were in my personal life as a believer.

I think, to some extent, the SU filled a gap that my local church at the time did not satisfy, until a year on when I met another young man, who had just been baptised with fire to start a revival among young people in my local church.

This person, whom I called my counsellor, helped me grasp the weightier matters of the scriptures. He held series of meetings for young people outside of school term times. So, by divine order, I was helped to thrive in God's presence at both ends! More than ever, Church life became paramount in my life, both in the boarding house, during term times, and at home during vacations. All-night sessions, half-night sessions, retreats and prayer meetings were all in the mix for me as a teenager, and I enjoyed being a part!

I graduated to become a co-worker in this youth ministry which, by God's grace, drew many young lives to the saving knowledge of God. I served as the leader of the music ministry, *Golden Praise Team*. By working hard in the grace of God, I found my place; I got clarity about my purpose and vision. I knew I was a worshipper! I still remember the first spoken prophesy I received to confirm my calling into the worship ministry, which also affirmed my own inner witnesses (I was in the first year of Sixth Form, about 17-18 years old).

Things even got bigger and better! The person, who God used to spark a shift in my life later became my husband! *(The story of my married life is potentially another book on its own!).*

CHAPTER TEN

IT'S ALL ABOUT JESUS!

Indeed, from the Old Testament all the way to the New, the focus of worship is Christ! He alone is and would always be the keystone. A study of His ancestry shows how God planned everything to be based on Him, even from the foundations of the earth. Let us see what was written in the books of beginnings about Hm:

> [8]Judah, your brothers will praise you; your hand will be on the neck of your enemies; your father's sons will bow down to you.
>
> [9]You are a lion's cub, Judah; you return from the prey, my son. Like a lion he crouches and lies down, like a lioness—who dares to rouse him?

> [10]The scepter will not depart from Judah, nor the ruler's staff from between his feet, until he to whom it belongs shall come and the obedience of the nations shall be his.
>
> [11]He will tether his donkey to a vine, his colt to the choicest branch; he will wash his garments in wine, his robes in the blood of grapes.
>
> **Genesis 49:8-11 NIV**

This scripture affirms Christ's ancestry. However, the writer of Hebrews makes it clear that it is His priestly and divine nature that makes His status more solidified and unchallengeable:

> [16]One who has become a priest not on the basis of a regulation as to his ancestry but on the basis of the power of an indestructible life.
>
> [17]For it is declared: "You are a priest forever, in the order of Melchizedek."
>
> **Hebrews 7:16-17**

It is all about Jesus! This is the message God has been passing on to mankind, from Genesis to Revelation, in diverse ways and ultimately through the cross, that reconciliation with God and acceptable worship is not possible apart from Him. We have to "go through" Christ, the Author (first gate) and the Finisher (the veil before entering the Holy of Holies). Do you have His life? Are you truly born again? *"By your fruits you shall be known"* (Matthew 7:16a).

From our overview of the Tabernacle, we learnt that the gate is the only access into the Tabernacle. Is it possible that some have attempted to "sneak" into the "Tabernacle" (the church) through other means? Do we have those who have "jumped" the white linen walls and found their way into the courts or the Holy place just to merely "have fun" with each other, rather than God? Some have not even received the message of the gospel or had an encounter with Christ at the gate. This is why many people struggle to live the Christian lives.

If you are yet to encounter Christ, the Gate, the Way that leads to the Father, I invite you to pray the *Salvation Prayer* on page 67.

On the other hand, you may need to rededicate your life to Christ and ask for the fire of His Spirit to rekindle your devotional life. It is important that Christ takes His rightful place in your life and for the passion of intimacy to burn brightly as you give your all in worship.

Therefore, let us hear the conclusion of the whole matter: it is all about Him, the Son of God, lifted up will bring all men to Himself! When spiritual worship goes up, we will see RESULTS.

I pray that the inspiration and direction you have received from of this book will catapult your worship life to another level, higher than you used to be. I also pray that at the coming of the Messiah, when we see Him face to face, we shall be rewarded for offering holy, undiluted and acceptable worship and praise that brought results.

I will leave you with one of my favourites, which I believe God likes too!

Jesus, the Son of God is lifted high

The Son of God is lifted High
(The Son of God is lifted High)
The Son of God is lifted High
(The Son of God is lifted High)

Oh wonderful and Glorious
Jesus the Son of God is lifted High
Oh wonderful and Glorious
Jesus the Son of God is lifted
The son of God is magnified
(The son of God is magnified)

The son of God is magnified
(The son of God is magnified)

In Nigeria put your location), Jesus is magnified
(The son of God is magnified)
In my life, Jesus is magnified
(The son of God is magnified)
(Lyrics by Nathaniel Bassey)

Love always!

Your Worship Partner and God's Handmaiden,

Minister Becky!

***iFlourish Media** is a Christian Ministry that seeks to explore the concept of Worship and Devotional Life from biblical perspective (the Word). Our foundational Scripture is from Psalm 92:13, which states: "Those that be planted in the house of the LORD shall **flourish** in the courts of our God."*

OUR CORE FOCI ARE:

Worship and Praise:

"But thou art holy, O thou that inhabitest the praises of Israel". (Ps 22:3). If we want God to dwell in our situations, then we MUST lead a WORSHIPFUL life.

Word:

"And it shall come to pass afterward, that I will pour out my spirit upon all flesh; and your sons and your daughters shall prophesy". (Joel 2:28 a&b). All God's children are anointed to preach His Word!

Witnessing:

"And he said unto them, go ye into all the world, and preach the gospel to every creature." Mark 16:15. Jesus commands us to spread the Good News!

What's On:

"But know this, that in the last days, critical times, hard to deal with will be here" (2 Timothy 3:1). We constantly trust God for the grace to interpret happenings around the world through the scriptures to provide alertness for the second coming of Christ.

To this end, I am available to partner with you and your group to lift the banner of Jesus higher, through:

- WORSHIP LEADING & OR SONG MINISTRATIONS
- WORSHIP TEACHINGS & SEMINARS
- PREACHING AND TEACHING THE WORD.

For more information, contact:

rebeccaiflourishministries@gmail.com

NOTES

NOTES

NOTES

NOTES

NOTES

NOTES